For:

CELTIC LIGHT

WISDOM & LORE

WRITTEN AND COMPILED
BY CLAUDINE GANDOLFI

PETER PAUPER PRESS, INC.
WHITE PLAINS, NEW YORK

*To those who never
stop longing with their very
being–you never know.*

Book design by Theresa Fitzgerald
All photographs courtesy Corbis,
used by permission
Title page - Adam Woolfitt
Page 4-5 - Richard Cummins
Page 11 - Michael St. Maur Sheil
Page 16 - Michael St. Maur Sheil
Page 21 - Richard Cummins
Page 24 - Michael St. Maur Sheil
Page 34 - Adam Woolfitt
Page 39 - Richard Cummins
Page 44-45 - Galen Rowell
Page 49 - Richard Cummins
Page 54-55 - Adam Woolfitt
Page 59 - Adam Woolfitt
Page 63 - Adam Woolfitt
Page 64 - Michael St. Maur Sheil

CONTENTS

INTRODUCTION

Celtic (KEL-tic) legends are filled with all the attributes that the Celts held in esteem: a sense of the extraordinary, admiration of nature in all her forms, exaggeration, love, plenty of laughter, hospitality, a heightened spirituality, bravado, a sense of adventure, and a fierce desire for expression.

These often incredible tales have been preserved through oral tradition; in fact, early Druidic teachings taught that nothing sacred could be written down. The telling of tales was one way the Celts kept alive their love of the magical and mysterious, as they migrated from the Rhine River valleys through Northern Italy and into France, before finally settling in the British Isles. It wouldn't be until the later Middle Ages, when Irish monks copied down these oral tales, that a set collection of some of the most revered "sacred history" of the Celts came into being. While continental Europe was experiencing a "Dark Age," the illuminated manuscripts of these monks shed light on the knowledge and learning that the Celts had accumulated over the centuries.

Who were the Celts? Today, their descendants live in Ireland and Scotland and on The Isle of Man (the Gaelic-speaking branch), and in Wales, Brittany, and Cornwall (the Brythonic-speaking branch). They are, however, more easily defined by their language than by their residence or lineage. Woven beautifully into their bardic tales, as knotwork is woven into Celtic crosses and decoration, is a strong sense of nature and the natural, and this stems from a sense of connection to the earth. Although we might think of Celts as tartaned, iron-wielding warriors, they were actually more at home farming the land.

Celtic love and life are infused with spirituality. Initially pagan, the Celts possessed a natural spirituality that effortlessly melded with Christianity, yet still retained a Celtic strain. The lyrical innocence of the body and spirit as one, a strong connection to the natural world, and a belief in the immortality of the soul were already in Celtic consciousness.

As is apparent in their legends, the Celts believed in the equality of the sexes. Female deities were prevalent in pre-Christian Celtic mythology, and the Celts never lost their respect and reverence for women. In Celtic legends, heroines are much more likely to be fiery and strong-willed than to be weak-kneed and passive.

The tales that follow are all Celtic in that each originated from a Celtic-speaking people. The bit of Celtic wisdom that follows each legend illuminates Celtic qualities that are manifest in the tale.

DEIRDRE
(Irish)

In this mournful tale of star-crossed love, it is clear that no matter what outside actions affect Deirdre (of the sorrows) she possesses a strength that does not falter. This tale incorporates some of the attributes that the Celts most valued–bravery, hospitality, and sensuality–and some cherished themes–the role of the supernatural, the power of nature, and reincarnation. Note that Cathbad the Druid functions as mystic, guardian, and teacher. Trees were revered as gods by pre-Christian Celts; their permanence suggested a sense of immortality. The yew tree in particular is significant because it is evergreen, everliving, thereby imparting a sense of continuity and peace to the tale.

Felim, one of the lords of Ulster, graced King Conchobhar with a grand feast. During the celebrations and festivities, the heroes of the Red Branch warriors delighted over roasted meat, cakes, and wine. In the midst of the merry-making, a messenger brought news that Felim's wife had just blessed him with a baby daughter. Each of the lords and their men offered up a toast, blessing the newborn babe.

King Conchobhar, extending his good graces, offered Felim the services of Cathbad, his Druid companion. Cathbad, being skilled in divination, agreed to foretell the future of the child. Cathbad's news was not, however, what the assemblage had expected. He divined that a great sadness would befall the kingdom: "This newborn babe with golden curls, peaceful grey eyes, and rosy complexion," he said, "may have the appearance of an angel, but her marriage will bring death and destruction to the fighting men of Ulster."

The men in the banquet hall called for the baby's immediate death. They would have none destroy their kingdom. But King Conchobhar forbade such action. "I will prevent the doom," he said, "for she shall wed no foreign king, but she shall be my own bride when she is of age." The king took the child into his custody, provided her with a nurse, Levarcam, and named her Deirdre.

The king charged Levarcam with raising the child in the woods in solitude, and instructed the woman to prevent the child from ever being seen by, or seeing, any young man. Deirdre was raised happily in the forest with Levarcam and Cathbad, and occasionally the old King, as her protectors.

One crisp winter day, as the time for Deidre's marriage to King Conchobhar drew near, she and Levarcam were exploring the ramparts of her fortress. A heavy snow had fallen during the night, leaving the trees sealed in a silvery icy casing. The whole meadow was blanketed in a serene white covering except for a small area in which a worker had slaughtered a calf, where the snow lay stained with blood. Deirdre's eyes were riveted to the spot. A raven darted down from a nearby tree and began to drink the spilled blood of the calf.

Deirdre, transfixed, exclaimed to her nurse: "Oh, this is the manner of man I would wed, not King Conchobhar. One whose hair is as black as a raven's wing and whose cheek has the hue of blood with a body as white as the snow." Levarcam smiled, for she loved the girl so and did not want her married to the old king. "Your desires can yet be made real," the nurse said. "The one you speak of is Naoise, son of Usna, and a champion of the Red Branch." Deirdre pleaded with the old woman to take her to see Naoise, and so she did.

Naoise, however, would not betray his king. He had heard of the prophecy at Deirdre's birth and wanted nothing to do with her–that is, until she implored him to save her from King Conchobhar. Her beauty and charm won him over, and he vowed to be hers. Secretly, Naoise and two of his brothers, Ardan and Ainle, shuttled Deirdre and Levarcam to a ship bound for Scotland. Away to the Pictish King they sailed, eluding King Conchobhar's soldiers. But they could never rest. Wherever they went, Conchobhar sought Deirdre. He made several attempts to kidnap her from Naoise, her true love. Eventually, Naoise and Deirdre settled in Glen Etive where they built a wild wood dwelling and spent their time hunting, fishing, and keeping to themselves.

With the passing of the seasons, King Conchobhar ceased to cause the lovers grief, but he was simply biding his time. Judging that Naoise would soon be complacent in his new life, Conchobhar sent Fergus Mac Roth, Naoise's best friend, to entice them to return under his protection. Joyfully did Fergus extend the alms of peace and joyfully did Naoise receive them. But not so Deirdre, who sensed ill intent on the king's part. Naoise refused to countenance her suspicions and chastised her for her doubts. And so they traveled back home with Fergus, under the protection of the Irish King.

Upon landing in Ireland, they were met by Baruch, a lord of the Red Branch, who invited Fergus to his nearby fortress for a feast. Fergus expressed his desire to continue home with Deirdre and Naoise to Emain Macha, but Baruch insisted on showing Fergus his hospitality. Still uneasy, Deirdre begged Fergus not to leave them. Fergus could not be dissuaded, but he put his sons, Illan the Fair and Buino the Red, in charge of Deirdre's and Naoise's passage home.

The lovers arrived at Emain Macha in the bosom of the Red Branch's kingdom. They were well received, but not by the king. After the evening meal, Conchobhar summoned Levarcam to him. "How goes it with the sons of Usna?" he asked. Levarcam was not easily duped and spun a tale to enlighten the king. "All goes well. You have the three bravest champions in all of Ulster back in your court. Truly, the king who has these three need fear no enemy." Conchobhar thought about what she had said. "How goes it with Deirdre?" he then asked. "She is well," Levarcam responded, trying to dissuade the king from his intent. "But she has toiled many years in the woods, and hardship has changed her. Little of her beauty now remains, my king." Conchobhar then dismissed Levarcam and continued drinking.

Eventually, Conchobhar called his servant Trendorn and sent him to spy on all in attendance at the Red Branch House. When he arrived at Red Branch House, Trendorn could not gain entrance because the place was bolted and barred. But he was eager to please his king and took a nearby ladder and ascended to peek through a high window. There he saw the brothers of Naoise and the sons of Fergus sharing tales as they cleaned their weapons and prepared for a night's sleep. Then, to the side, he spotted Naoise complacently playing chess with the fairest woman he had ever seen. As Trendorn stood captivated by Deirdre's unsurpassed beauty, he was seen by one of the ladies, who sounded the alarm. Naoise was infuriated and grabbed one of the chess pieces, flinging it at Trendorn. So great was the strength with which he hurled the piece that it put out Trendorn's eye.

The bloodied spy returned to his king to report. "I have seen all of them," he bellowed. "I have seen the fairest woman in all the world. Had Naoise not struck my eye out,

I would still be gazing upon her!"

Conchobhar called his guards and sent them to charge the sons of Usna with maiming the messenger of the king. They were met by Buino, Fergus's son, and his retinue, who drove them back with the sharp steel of their swords. All the while, Naoise and Deirdre continued their chess game. Naoise believed that it would not be fitting to defend himself while they were under the protection of the sons of Fergus. However, the king was not about to give up. He secretly went to Buino and offered him huge tracts of land in exchange for deserting his charge. Buino accepted the bribe. That left the lovers' defense up to Illan, who was dispatched by two of the king's sons. Betrayed and left unaided, Naoise and his brothers at last met with the king's men in battle. Many were killed.

The king, sensing that the lovers would

escape, entreated Cathbad, the Druid, to use his skills of conjuring in order to prevent their flight. The king vowed that he would not harm the two if they were taken alive. So Cathbad invoked a lake of ooze to appear under the feet of the sons of Usna. Trapped in the mire, they could not flee, and the guards captured them and brought them before King Conchobhar. Knowing that Naoise stood between him and Deirdre, the king ordered each of his men to come forward and slay the captured sons of Usna–but all refused. Finally, Owan, son of Duracht and Prince of Ferney, took the sword of Naoise and with one fell swoop beheaded the three brothers. Deirdre's beloved was no more. The kingdom was in a shambles and 3,000 men were banished, fulfilling Cathbad's prophecy.

For a year, Deirdre was forced to live with the king at the palace in Emain Macha. With Naoise dead, she would never smile again.

This drove the king to distraction. "Tell me, Deirdre," he said, "what is it that you hate most on all of God's green earth?" Scornfully she spat, "You and Owan, son of Duracht." "Then I will give you to Owan," the king declared. Silently Deirdre mounted the chariot behind Owan and kept her eyes locked on the ground, because she would not look into the eyes of her tormentors. But the king taunted her again by saying: "Deirdre, the sight of you between Owan and me is that of a ewe caught between two rams!" Unwilling to face the life that awaited her, Deirdre rose from the chariot and flung herself, headfirst, onto the rocky passage.

A yew sprouted on the spot where they laid Deidre to rest. From Naoise's grave, on the other side of Armagh Church, another yew grew. And these two trees entwined over the roof of the church and no one could part them again, ever.

WISDOM

Death is never the conqueror and we are reminded that the Celts were one of the first cultures to evolve a sophisticated doctrine of the immortality of the soul.

PETER BERRESFORD ELLIS

I arise today
    Through the strength of heaven:
Light of sun,
    Radiance of moon,
Splendour of fire,
    Speed of lightning,
Swiftness of wind,
    Depth of sea,
Stability of earth,
    Firmness of rock.

THE DEER'S CRY
attributed to St. Patrick,
7th century (Trans. Meyer)

*O, that the great sea would dry up to
make a way, that I may go through: the
snow of Greenland shall grow red like
roses before I can forget my love.*

MANX TRADITIONAL
(Trans. Jackson)

*The Celtic affinity with nature in all her
aspects, along with respect for the sea-
sonal festivals, equality of the sexes
and other important issues, is bringing
new light into a declining system.*

DAVID JAMES

TRYSTAN AND ESYLLT

(Welsh)

Many are familiar with the tale of Tristan and Isolde from the Arthurian legends telling of a love that was all-consuming, yet never meant to be. This excerpt, from a 16th-century Welsh manuscript, traces the competition between Trystan and King March of Cornwall, rather than the tale of the two lovers. King Arthur provides justice worthy of Solomon, in a manner particularly suited to Trystan's Celtic sense of wit and play.

Esyllt, the betrothed of King March ap Meirchion, eloped with Trystan to escape the king's wrath. With their servants, they fled into the woods of Kelyddon. King March protested to King Arthur and set out with his armies to hunt down the wayward Trystan and recapture Esyllt. Three of March's armies were overcome by the heroic Trystan.

At March's request, King Arthur agreed to intervene between the factions. Tristan appeared before Arthur and was given the king's noble judgment on the dilemma. Arthur decreed that since both men had a claim to Esyllt they must share her. One would be hers during that part of the year in which the trees have leaves and the other when they are bare.

Since King March was the one who was initially to be Esyllt's husband, he was offered first choice. He chose the winter, slyly reasoning that the nights are longer during this time. So, the decision was made and Arthur's command given. But Trystan pointed out that the yew tree is evergreen, never losing its leaves. Therefore, March could never be with Esyllt because there is never a time when all trees are bare.

WISDOM

Celtic spiritual wholeness is defined by three conditions: cràbhadh–*the trust of the soul, or devout observance;* creideamh–*the heart's consent, or belief;* iris–*the mind's pledge, or faith.*

CAITLÍN MATTHEWS

In the Celtic world, and especially in the Celtic world of the senses, there was no barrier between soul and body. Each was natural to the other. The soul was the sister of the body, the body the sister of the soul. As yet there was no negative splitting of dualistic Christian morality, which later did so much damage to these two lovely and enfolded presences. The world of Celtic consciousness enjoyed this unified and lyrical sensuous spirituality.

JOHN O'DONOHUE

TALIESIN
(Welsh)

Taliesin (Tal-i-ES-in) is the bard of leg-end. This legend of "shining brow" demon-strates the Celtic love of magic, learning, and the rebirth of the soul, the gift of spinning tales, and a cunning sense of humor. The Celtic cauldron, used here by Ceridwen, is a symbol of magic and an archetype of the Holy Grail. King Arthur's bardic contest reminds one of the Eisteddfod, a major cultural festi-val in Wales with contests in poetry and music. Celtic bards were the highest-ranking officials at court. The duties of the poet included inspiring people, encouraging them, and entertaining them. They were the keepers of the heroic cycles, songs, proverbs, and tra-ditions; and the semi-mythical Taliesin was the greatest of them all.

In the days when Arthur and his knights

ruled Britain, there lived a bard named Taliesin, who was the foremost storyteller ever to walk the earth. This is the story of how he received his talent:

The sorceress Ceridwen (Celtic goddess of inspiration) had a son named Avagddu, who happened to be the most repulsive-looking man on earth. In an attempt to compensate for his lack of physical beauty by making him wise above all others, Ceridwen prepared a magic brew in a cauldron. In it she placed that which would grant knowledge of all that had come before, the magic of transmutation, insight into the human heart, and prophecy of what yet would be. Only three drops of the liquid that the cauldron contained would be of use. Gwion Bach was to stir the cauldron for one year and Morda, a blind man, was to ensure that the flames were kept lit.

One day, toward the end of that year,

three drops escaped the cauldron and land-
ed on the fingertips of the servant, Gwion
Bach. Licking his fingers, Gwion was graced
with instantaneous supernatural insight.
Sensing that he had received what Ceridwen
had intended for her ugly son, Gwion fled, to
avoid being destroyed by Ceridwen. Now
deprived of its magic, the potion turned to
poison that burst the cauldron, flooded a
river, and killed the horses of Gwyddno
Garanhir.

When Ceridwen discovered what had
happened, she killed poor Morda instantly
and set upon finding Gwion. Gwion changed
himself into a hare. Ceridwen pursued him
as a greyhound, whereupon Gwion dove into
a river and became a fish. Ceridwen then
turned herself into an otter. On and on this
cycle continued until Gwion hid himself as a
grain of wheat on a threshing floor.
Ceridwen, now a black hen, devoured him.
Nine months later she bore him as a child.

Though she fully intended to destroy the child, Ceridwen found she could not because he was so beautiful. Instead, she wrapped him in a leather sack and cast the babe into the sea, leaving his fate in the hands of God.

One day Elphin, Gwyddno's unlucky son, found the sack and the infant within. He named the child Taliesin and raised him. When Taliesin was a youth, he praised Elphin in his very first poem, causing Elphin to be favored with King Arthur. But in time the always boastful Elphin proclaimed that he had a wife more virtuous than any at Arthur's court and a bard more talented! These boasts angered the king and the braggart Elphin was cast into prison until he could prove his claims.

Elphin was held prisoner with a silver chain around his feet. Rhun was sent to seduce Elphin's wife. It was rumored that any woman who came into contact with

Rhun gained a bad reputation. But Taliesin knew what was being plotted and instructed Elphin's wife to disguise herself and to have the kitchen maid bear herself like her mistress. So mistress went about in maid's clothing and maid in mistress's. When Rhun arrived, the maid greeted him and he plied her with drink. While she slept, he cut the ring finger, which bore Elphin's signet, off her left hand and brought it back to Arthur's court.

The following morning Elphin was brought out of prison and shown the severed finger and ring as proof of his wife's infidelity. "First, I cannot deny that this is my signet ring, mighty king. But the finger it is on is not my wife's. The ring fits quite tightly on this finger while the ring was even too large for my wife to wear on her thumb. Second, my wife grooms her nails once each week, whereas this nail hasn't been cut or shaped in well over a month. Third, whomever this

finger belonged to was used to kneading rye-dough, but my wife hasn't touched rye-dough as long as she's been alive." This glib response angered the king even more and he threw Elphin back into prison.

On the day that the king's bards and minstrels would sing and play for the court, Taliesin hid quietly in a corner as the others went about entertaining the court. In the midst of a performance he puckered his lips and mimed "Blerwm, blerwm" with his finger on his mouth as a child does. And from then on, whenever the bards tried to perform, "Blerwm, blerwm" was all that they could utter! Heinin, the foremost storyteller, prostrated himself before the king, and said: "Oh king, we're not all drunk with wine, but are struck dumb through the trickery of the spirit who sits in the corner under the guise of a child!" So, Taliesin was brought to the king and was asked who he was. Taliesin sang his response. It was a tale equating his life to that of Merlin, an account of witnessing recorded history since the fall of Lucifer.

The castle shook with the rages of a great thunderstorm and Arthur knew Elphin had been vindicated. The king had Elphin brought before the court, and Taliesin sang a song so lovely that Elphin's shackles magically fell off. Elphin regained his freedom.

WISDOM

We should never forget that quality of mischievous fun that runs throughout [Celtic myths]. They are meant to be enjoyed as well as learnt from.

PETER BERRESFORD ELLIS

Hearing the stories [of the bards] was more than entertainment. Those who listened attentively were promised health, wealth, progeny, freedom from captivity, safe voyage, and protection.

ELLEN EVERT HOPMAN

[Celts] are inclined to desert the natural and possible for the impossible and supernatural, chiefly in the form of fantastic exaggeration. One should not misunderstand this, however; it was not done in all seriousness, but for its own sake, for the fun of the thing.

KENNETH JACKSON

I am the child of poetry,
   Poetry, the child of Reflection,
Reflection, the child of Meditation,
   Meditation, the child of Lore,
Lore, the child of Research,
   Research, the child of Great
   Knowledge,
Great Knowledge, the child of
Intelligence,
   Intelligence, the child of
   Understanding,
Understanding, the child of Wisdom,
   Wisdom, the child of the three gods
   of Danu.

COLLOQUY OF THE TWO SAGES
(Irish)

TAM LIN

(Scottish)

Tam Lin is the story of Janet, who through the strength of her will captured an enchanted knight. This old Scottish ballad, set down in an anthology by Francis James Child, includes references to Celtic well magic. Wells were known as the thresholds between worlds and possessed a magic of their own. The Celtic feast of Samhain (SOW-in), known to us as Halloween, was the time when the passageways to the faery world were opened. There are also references in the poem to Christian baptism, steadfast love, and transmigration of the soul. Janet's green mantle (cloak) is a symbol of faery magic. Only those on good terms with the faery could wear green without retribution. Green is also the color of fertility.

O I forbid you, maidens all,
That wear gold on your hair,
To come or go by Carterhaugh,
For young Tam Lin is there.

There's none that go by Carterhaugh
But they leave him a wad[1],
Either their rings, or green mantles,
Or else their maidenhead.

Janet has tucked up her green skirts
A little above her knee,
And she has braided her yellow hair
A little above her eye
And she's away to Carterhaugh
As fast as she can flee.

When she came to Carterhaugh
Tam Lin was at the well,
And there she found his steed standing,
But away was himself.

She had not plucked a double rose,
A rose but not yet two,
Till up then started young Tam Lin,

[1] wad=gift or something of great value

Says, "Lady, no more pluck you.

"Why pluck you the rose, Janet,
And why break you the wand?[2]
Or why come you to Carterhaugh
Without my command?"

"Carterhaugh, it is my own,
My daddy gave it me,
I'll come and go by Carterhaugh,
And ask no leave of thee."

Janet has tucked up her green skirts
A little above her knee,
And she has braided her yellow hair
A little above her eye
And she is to her father's hall,
As fast as she can flee.

Four and twenty ladies fair
Were playing at the ball,
And out then came the fair Janet,
The flower among them all.

Four and twenty ladies fair

<hr>

[2] wand=stem

Were playing at the chess,
And out then came the fair Janet,
As green as any glass.[3]

Out then spoke an old grey knight,
Lay over the castle wall,
And says, "Alas, fair Janet, for thee,
But we'll be blamed all."

"Hold your tongue, you old fac'd knight,
Some ill death may you die!
I'll father my babe on whom I will,
I'll father none on thee."

Out then spoke her father dear,
And he spoke meek and mild,
"And ever alas, sweet Janet,"
    he says,
"I think you are with child."

"If that I am with child, father,
Myself must bear the blame,
There's not a lord about your hall,
Shall give the child his name.

[3] green as glass=looking green, sickly

"If my love were an earthly knight,
As he's an elven grey,
I would not give my own true-love
For any lord that you say.

"The steed that my true love
    rides on
Is lighter than the wind,
With silver he is shod before,
With burning gold behind."

Janet has tucked up her green skirts
A little above her knee,
And she has braided her yellow hair
A little above her eye
And she's away to Carterhaugh
As fast as she can flee.

When she came to Carterhaugh,
Tam Lin was at the well,
And there she found his steed standing,
But away was himself.

She had not plucked a double rose,
A rose but not yet two,

Till up then started young Tam Lin,
Says, "Lady, no more pluck you.

"Why plucks thou the rose, Janet,
Among the groves so green,
And all to kill the bonny babe
That we made us between?"

"O tell me, tell me, Tam Lin," she says,
"For's sake that died on tree,[4]
If ever you were in holy chapel,
Or Christendom did see?"

"Roxbrugh he was my grandfather,
Took me with him to wait
And by chance it fell upon a day
That woe for me was fate.

"And by chance it fell upon a day
A cold day and a snell,[5]
When we were from the
   hunting come,
That from my horse I fell,
The Queen of Fairies she caught me,
In that green hill to dwell.

[4] died on tree=died on the cross, Christ
[5] snell=piercing, windy

"And pleasant is the fairy land,
But, an eerie tale to tell,
Aye, at the end of seven years,
We pay a tax to hell,
I am so fair and full of flesh,
I'm fear it is myself.

"But the night is Halloween, lady,
The morn is Hallowday,
Then win me, win me, and you will,
For will I what you may.

"Just at the dark and midnight hour
The fairy folk will ride,
And they that would their true-love win,
At Miles Cross they must bide."

"But how shall I know you, Tam Lin,
Oh how my true-love know,
Among so many unknown knights,
The like I never saw?"

"O first let pass the black, lady,
And then let pass the brown,
But quickly run to the milk-white steed,

Pull you his rider down.

"For I'll ride on the milk-white steed,
And nearest to the town,
Because I was an earthly knight
They grant me that renown.

"My right hand will be gloved, lady,
My left hand will be bare,
Tilted shall my own hat be,
And combed down shall my hair,
By these tokens I give thee,
Don't doubt I will be there.

"They'll turn me in your arms, lady,
Into a newt and adder,
But hold me fast, and fear me not,
I am your child's father.

"They'll turn me to a bear so grim,
And then a lion bold,
But hold me fast, and fear me not,
And you shall love your child.

"Again they'll turn me in your arms

To an iron rod, red hot,
But hold me fast, and fear me not,
Harm I'll do you not.

"And last they'll turn me in your arms
Into the burning coal,
Then throw me into well water,
O throw me in with speed.

"And then I'll be your own true-love,
I'll turn a naked knight,
Then cover me with your green mantle,
And hide me out of sight."

Gloomy, gloomy was the night,
And eerie was the way,
As fair Jenny in her green mantle
To Miles Cross she did go.

At the dark and midnight hour
She heard the bridles sing,
She was as glad at that
As any earthly thing.

First she let the black pass by,
And then she let the brown,

*But quickly she ran to the milk-white
    steed,*
And pulled the rider down.

So well she followed what he did say,
And young Tam Lin did win,
Then covered him with her green mantle,
As blythe's a bird in spring.

Out then spoke the Queen of Fairies,
Out of a bush of broom,
"She that has gotten young Tam Lin
Has gotten a stately-groom."

Out then spoke the Queen of Fairies,
And an angry woman was she,
"Shame befall her ill-faired face,
And an ill death may she die,
*For she's taken away the bonniest
    knight*
In all my company.

"Had I but known, Tam Lin," said she,
"What now this night I see,
I would have taken out your two grey eyes,
And put in two even of tree."[6]

---

[6] tree=wood, so that Tam Lin would never have seen Janet

WISDOM

Water was the mystical entranceway to the Otherworld, and offerings would be thrown into wells and lakes as gifts for the Gods and Goddesses.

ELLEN EVERT HOPMAN

The trinity of the soul, heart and mind are strong in harmony, yet they can be shattered if they are not in union. Doubt, distrust and neglected observances are the pathways to madness, heartsickness and soul fragmentation.

CAITLÍN MATTHEWS

A false love is the love of men—woe to the woman who does their will! Though their fine talk is sweet, their hearts are hidden deep within.

IRISH, 15TH CENTURY
(Trans. Jackson)

The women, who were held in high regard, were as good warriors as their men. Any Celtic woman with her temper aroused was a dangerous force to be reckoned with. In early Celtic history, it was not unusual for women to fight alongside their men.

D. J. CONWAY

One of the amazing aspects of the Celtic world is the idea of shape shifting. This becomes possible only when the physical is animate and passionate. . . . Soul has a fluency and energy that is not to be caged within any fixed form. Consequently, in the Celtic tradition there is a fascinating interflow between soul and matter and between time and eternity.

JOHN O'DONOHUE

The sacred and the secular worlds were not seen as being in opposition to each other, but rather as part of the whole.

PETER GLANVILLE

ST. BRIGIT
(Irish)

St. Brigit is truly a bridge between the old and the new, a link between pagan and Christian Celtic spirituality. The ancient goddess Brighid (also known as Dana or Danu) was the mother of poetry, healing, light, knowledge, and smithcraft, and, at the same time, the Saint and foster mother of Christ. She is the embodiment of the Celtic spiritual "oneness," a unity which supplants Christian duality of body and soul and the triune nature of God. To the Irish, she is St. Brigit; to the Welsh, St. Ffraid; to the Scots, St. Bride, but to all she is the one who illumines the darkness.

This 5th-century Irish saint, St. Brigit of Kildare, although Ireland's only native patron saint, ranks second to St. Patrick as patron and protector of Ireland. Raised in a Druidic household, she founded an abbey in Kildare to maintain a sacred fire, which was tended by 19 nuns. The sacred flame burned from the 5th century until the dissolution of the monasteries under the Reformation. St. Brigit is a model of compassion and steadfast love, offering the much-revered Celtic hospitality to travelers who reached her abbey.

Legend tells how St. Brigit came to the aid of the Holy Family in its darkest hour. During Candlemas (Imbolc), as Mary, Joseph, and the swaddled infant Jesus made their flight from Herod's soldiers, Brigit made a crown of candles, placed it upon her head and pranced around to distract the soldiers from capturing the Holy Family.

In other legends she is the foster mother of the Christ child, and is known as "the Mary of the Gael." Her protective mantle, or

cloak, is invoked to cure numerous ailments and overcome myriad difficulties. On her feast day, February 1st, Celts still celebrate her holiness by constructing Brigit's Crosses out of interlaced straw. These braided or woven crosses, which are hung near house doors as well as at entrances to barns and stables, are reminders of the beautiful Celtic crosses that through the centuries were decorated with patterned knotwork.

WISDOM

The weaving thread of Celtic knot-work symbolizes the soul's path through life, encoding certain qualities and powers into the object so decorated. These patterns are not mere decoration but meaningful pathways which hold soul-life and can help to lead it back when it strays.

CAITLIN MATTHEWS

Celtic Christianity was able to build on much raw material already in existence. It did not seek to stamp out an ancient culture which in many ways valued the sacred as a part of everyday life. The brand of Christianity which St.Columba spread was gentle and all-embracing. It absorbed those aspects of

paganism which were seen to be benefi-
cial.

PETER GLANVILLE

Light is incredibly generous, but also
gentle. When you attend to the way the
dawn comes, you learn how light can
coax the dark.

JOHN O'DONOHUE

Gold wears out, silver wears out, velvet
wears out, silk wears out, every ample
garment wears out—yet longing does not
wear out.

WELSH
(Trans. Jackson)